WHISPERS
IN GOD'S EAR

Children's Thoughts
From Their Hearts

Written and illustrated by
"The Prayer Children"

Abbey Press
St. Meinrad, IN 47577

MW01222065

Text ©2003 Saint Bernard School
Illustrations ©2003 Saint Bernard School
Published by Abbey Press
St. Meinrad, Indiana 47577

All rights reserved.
No part of this book may be used or reproduced in any manner without written
permission of the publisher, except in the case of brief quotations embodied in
critical articles and reviews.

Library of Congress Catalog Number
2003096173

ISBN 0-87029-377-X

Book design by Rita Marsili
Cover art by Megan, age 12
Printed in the United States of America

Table of Contents

"Let the children come to me."
—Mark 10:14

Foreword

I plant seeds. As the Director of Schools for the Diocese of Evansville, a 12-county area in Southwestern Indiana, I like to believe that planting seeds is part of my mission to ensure excellence for our schools. During the 18 years I have worked in the central office, I have pushed to "raise the bar" of excellence. In addition to this, I have tried to give the principals and teachers opportunities to be creative and think of ways to bring new life to our schools and to the students who grace us with their presence each day. I say this with great humility, because these administrators and teachers are the ones who toil the soil so that those seeds I plant will grow. They, then, bring in the harvest that makes our schools outstanding in every way.

Whispers in God's Ear grew from a seed like all good projects. In the summer of 2002, I came upon another wonderful book, *God's Photo Album*, by Shelly Mecum, and decided to share it with each of our principals at our first administrator meeting of the new school year. As the principals arrived at the meeting, they found a copy of the book at their place along with tropical punch, leis, and other reminders of Hawaii, where *God's Photo Album* originated. I wanted them to be as inspired as I was when I read it and to feel the excitement that is on every page of the book.

Paula Lattner, principal of Saint Bernard School in a small town called Rockport, was inspired. She and Shelly Mecum started corresponding, and each time Paula talked to Shelly I would get the latest report on how writing her own book with the students at Saint Bernard was indeed a possibility. I knew Paula and her enthusiasm quite well. I knew that when she said she was going to do something, you better believe her and get on board, or move out of her way.

Whispers in God's Ear is about listening to what is in the heart and whispers of children. It is about planting a seed, toiling the soil, watching the seedling grow, and reaping the harvest that isn't expressed in whispers at all, but rather in shouts of faith, hope, and love. I have learned in my 30 years in education that children often show us the way. They *believe* that God hears their prayers. They *hope* for the best in all things, and they *love*, with all their hearts. Perhaps that is why Jesus said, "Let the children come to me." I hope that after you read this book your whispered prayers will be said and heard like those of children.

—Phyllis Bussing, Ph.D.
Director of Schools
Diocese of Evansville

INTRODUCTION

"I have carved you on the palm of my hand."
—Isaiah 49:15

In order to inspire us at the beginning of a new school year, Dr. Phyllis Bussing, Director of Catholic Schools for the Diocese of Evansville, Indiana, gave each principal the book, *God's Photo Album.* Knowing that I had mounds of work waiting for me back at school, I sarcastically snickered to the principal sitting next to me, "Sure, I'm going to read this entire book tonight." It took me two weeks to start reading it.

It was a Sunday afternoon when I picked up the book. Before I finished reading half of the book, I sprang from the living room couch and ran to the phone. I called the bookstore and asked the clerk if they had six copies. They did. I jumped in my car, drove to the bookstore and purchased the books.

The next evening our Saint Bernard School Board met for their monthly meeting. Because I am the principal, I was expected to present my goals for the coming school year. My knees were shaking as I began talking. I informed the board members that the Indiana State Testing Scores for our school were wonderful but we needed to improve in Language Mechanics. I added that after the World Trade Center was attacked, many of our parents were affected by the economic downturn and enrollment had decreased by twenty students. We are such a small school that this decrease resulted in a substantial loss of tuition income.

Next, I presented the school goals: (1) To work with staff, students, and parents to improve student academic achievement in Language Arts, and (2) To launch a public relations campaign that would result in an increase in enrollment. It was at that moment that I began to lose my nerve. Fear made me think about abandoning my plan. Instead, I asked the board for their help in achieving these goals. After pulling the books from under the table I handed each Board member a book. I explained that *God's Photo Album* was about a small Catholic school in Hawaii whose teacher and children wrote the book to keep the school from closing. Finally, I asked them to read this book and listen to God speaking to them as they read it. They were to try to think of a school-wide literacy project that would: (1) be an authentic literary experience for the children, (2) let the children know that God is everywhere, and (3) produce a school identity that would help our enrollment grow.

I also gave this presentation to my teachers at our faculty meeting. In October our School Board agreed that we should write a book. It would be a collection of children's prayers. Our children began writing prayers and producing the artwork in January.

As we worked on the book, it became increasingly important to write the prayers. History was unfolding with tragedy after tragedy. First, just one year earlier, the terrorist attack on the World Trade Center shattered our feeling of security. Next, the Columbia Space Shuttle disaster brought home the loss of precious lives. Finally, the War in Iraq added to the fears of our children. Indeed this was becoming a very scary time for adults. And it was even more frightening for our children. They needed to pray. I asked them to write prayers from their hearts hoping that these prayers would help them to process the tragedies in their world.

Our children live in the small town of Rockport, Indiana, and in the surrounding areas in Spencer County. Saint Bernard School is located in the heart of downtown Rockport. It truly is the "heart" of Rockport. Our small school has that warm, "family" atmosphere. When someone joins our staff or enrolls in our school, we tell them that they have joined the "Saint Bernard Family." Grandparents and parents of many of our school's children attended Saint Bernard School. Most people know each other by their first names. When we need to plan any event or activity, our parents willingly and enthusiastically share their talents, materials, and time with us.

Opened in 1877 by the Sisters of Saint Benedict in Ferdinand, Indiana, Saint Bernard School is the only Catholic School in Spencer County. The parish's ministry serves the community with preschool, daycare, before and after school care, full day kindergarten, and elementary and middle school education for children in grades K-8. Twenty percent of our children are not Catholic. Saint Bernard Catholic School has remained open for over 125 years because of the will of God and the sheer determination and support of the parents and parishioners. Our enrollment increases and decreases like the swing of a pendulum. We had been in a downward swing for the past two years and we needed to reverse the swing.

Many times I tell people that Saint Bernard School is the best-kept secret of Spencer County. Our mission is to educate the whole child to serve the world as a responsible Christian. These wonderful children are always willing to help others in need in the school, the community, and the world. They prove this over and over by participating in service projects. They make us proud. Why wouldn't God want these children in tiny Rockport to become authors and artists?

As the year passed it started to dawn on me that this book was not my project nor was it just the school's project; it was God's work and we had a duty to make it happen for our children. I was reminded that this was God's plan. "These were His children, His teachers, and this was His school. It will be His book."

Then I remembered the words of Father William Deering, former Director of Worship for the Diocese. I asked him if he wanted to contribute to the book and he gave me this quote: "All prayer is initiated by God, all prayer comes from God." I didn't know how prophetic this message was until now. God had orchestrated this project before it even entered my mind. It truly is His work. This project would be successful because it came from God.

These thoughts brought many questions to my mind: Who could have inspired me to jump off that couch and buy six copies of *God's Photo Album?* Who gave me the idea to use that book for a springboard for our literacy project? God was whispering in our ears. Only God knew that our children needed to be lifted up by His Spirit to live in this time in history. It is His will that causes our children to realize a dream of becoming authors and artists. That is why the Saint Bernard School children will forever be known as "The Prayer Children." God has always had us in the palm of His hand. We listened to His whispers. I invite you to listen to God's whispers as you read this book. God holds you in the palm of His hand, too!

—Paula Lattner
Principal
Saint Bernard Catholic School

P.S. Every effort was made to try to have every student at Saint Bernard Catholic School contribute to this book either as an author or as an artist.

I. Peaceful Whispers

Chris, age 11

Dear God,
I would like to pray to stop all of the terrorism in our world so everybody can get along. Amen

—Jordan, age 10

Maisie,
Bret, age 11

O God,
When I look at the sky I can see You with my eye. When I see the mountains I think of how beautiful You made this earth. When I walk on the beach I can feel You. I can feel You from the water, sun and the sky.

—Jacob, age 11

Mac, age 11

Dear All-powerful God,
I ask in this prayer that You remember all who lost their lives in war fighting for the rights of their country. I ask You to be with their families and friends. It takes a lot of bravery to defend this country of ours. I ask that You give them a peaceful place in heaven.

–Ryan, age 14

Brooke, age 10

Andrew, age 11

Dear God,
   When I think of the sun, the warm sand, and the ocean, I think of You. I feel Your warm love for me as I have felt the warmth of the tropical sands on my feet and the sun as it warmed my face.
   When I think of flowers I think of You because You are always pretty and You are always fresh and sweet.
   When I think of homework I think of You because You are always right. If I would ask You one question it would be, "Will this world ever have peace?"
                                            —Layne, age 11

Quinton, age 11

God is a person that
comes down from heaven and helps people.
When you pray for someone not to get hurt
God will help him. God forgives us when we
do something bad.

If somebody is getting ready to die God will help him.
God is a person who died for us so we can live. God is a
person who loves us. If we are hurt God is there to help us.

If we cannot reach something God is there to help. If
we are lost God will help. If we are sick God will help. If
we are crying God will help us feel better. Thank You, God,
for beautiful days, people, toys, clothes, beds, pencils,
and paper. Thank You for all the things You did
for us.

—Malin, age 7

Brett, age 11

O God,
Destroy the guns of hatred. Help there to be peace in our world. Let war be no more. Give peace to all nations. Help the people. Amen.
—Haley, age 9

Dear God,
Please extend a blessing over our country while we deal with the war. Watch over our country and protect us from all harm. Also help us, our president, and his council to make the right choices. Bless the soldiers that we sent out and protect them from all harm. —Lexi, age 12

Sam, age 12

Bret, age 11

God,
With all Your awesome power, please help our troops defend our country. Help them and be with them. Help their families deal with the emotional stress. Help the generals make the right choices. Help the people overcome their fears. Amen.

—Sam, age 12

Dear God,
I love You. You listen to
our prayers. You give us
drinks and food. You love
all of us. You are in our
hearts.

—Erica, age 7

Jacob, age 11

II. Playful Whispers

Ashleigh, age 10

God,
I am going to
lose a tooth.

—Jessica, age 6

Maisie, age 10

God,
Please keep
everybody safe in
my soccer game

—Riley, age 6

Kegan, age 6

Kara, age 6

God,
Can You make my
stuffed leopard,
Spot safe?
—Kara, age 6

Dear God,
I'm sorry that my friend's dog died
but I'm glad my friend's Dad is OK. He had a heart
attack. I'll bet You didn't give her a *Guardian
Angel*, You gave my friend a *Guardian Dog*.
Amen.
—Maisie, age 10

David, age 12

Austin, age 7

Dear God,
Please let my team win first place in softball.
—Lauren, age 7

When I think of God I think of the St. Louis Rams winning the Super Bowl because God has the power to make them win.
—Andrew, age 11

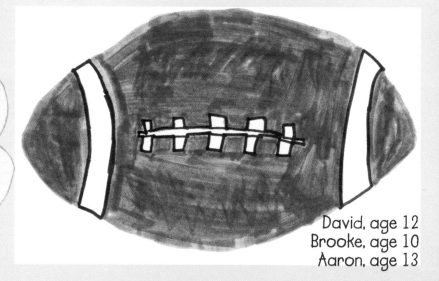

David, age 12
Brooke, age 10
Aaron, age 13

Matthew, age 9

Dear God,
I want to play in the sticky snow
While I watch the duck
That is stuck in the muck.
Thank You, God.

—Shayla age 8

Jared, age 9

I love You. I will be good to everyone. Will You make it a nice day, everyday? We don't have any money but Jesus gave us some. I will give everybody some presents.

—Keith, age 5

Thank You, God, for the snow day. I like snow days because we get school off. My brother and I can have a snowball fight.

—Jon, age 8

Amelia, age 8

Haley, age 8

Dear God, Will You watch over our puppet show? Thank You for making me a good actor in the puppet show.

—Macy, age 8

Dear God, Please help me play baseball better. Thank You very much.

—Davis, age 7

Ciara, age 7

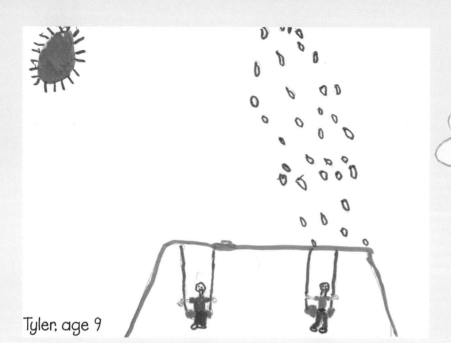

Tyler, age 9

Dear God,
Please can we have some more snow?
—Kegan, age 6

Dear God,
When I see the sunset, I think of You in all Your glory.
—Quinton, age 11

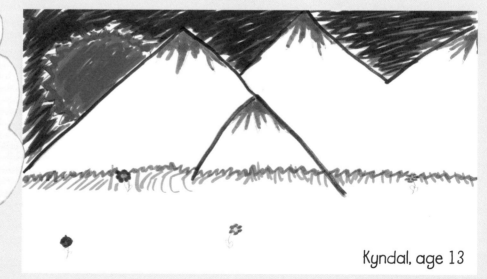

Kyndal, age 13

Dear God,
Please let me
do better in
basketball.
—Elicia, age 10

Keith, age 7

Oh Jesus,
How are You?
I don't like the
weather today. Please
change the weather
so it's summer. I would
like to play outside.
Please make the rain
stop.

—Curtis, age 8

Kara, age 6

Dear God,
When I see my classmates I see You because they are so joyful in everything they do especially the fifth graders.
When I think of trees I see You raising such a small seed into a great big tree. That's one of the miracles that You work. Amen.

—Brad, age 11

Layne, age 11

Dear God,
Thank you, God.
I love the things that You have given me in the lovely spring. Like the birds singing in the lovely spring breeze and the pretty blossoms that bloom right in front of me. Thank You, God, for everything. Amen.

—Alyssa, age 9

Elicia, age 10

III. Purposeful Whispers

Preston, age 11

Sarah, age 13

Dear God,
Something I love fits like a glove. It keeps me warm in the cold, and it protects me from harm. Something I love is always above and has a bird's eye view of everyone. Do You know who it is? It's You God.
—Justin, age 14

Dear God,
Please help other people to understand that they need to come to church and pray.
—Brooke, age 10

Chelsea, age 12

I love You God!
I will always listen to You.
I will do whatever You say.
Thank You for the world.
God is good all the time!

—Kaleb, age 5

Malin, age 6

Cayleigh, age 10

God is loving because He gives us food and drinks. I love God. I hope you do too. I think everyone loves God. He is in your heart. He gave his life for us. I love God. I hope you do too. He is in your heart. He gave his life for us.

—Regina, age 7

Oh God,
Please help the people in Haiti to have good water and something else besides rice and beans. Love,

—Kyle, age 8

Kaylea, age 6

Alyssa, age 9

Dear Lord Jesus Christ,
The snow has fallen and I heard that Saint Bernard School was not having school tomorrow. Please just let it snow a little bit so we can go to school. Amen.

—Riley, age 8

Derek, age 6

Dear God,
Help those who are
mean to others! Please help
the people who do right to
ignore those who are mean
to them! Amen.

—Brooke, age 10

I hope God will
keep my dog safe.

—Taylor, age 6

Maisie, age 10

God,
Forgive the sin I made. It's time for reconciliation.
—Colton, age 9

Jacob, age 11

Dear God,
    Please let all the countries in
the world end all the fighting.
    God, will You please let more
peace come into this world of ours?
God, will You also let the military
personnel to not get in any arguments. I
also pray for all the things on Earth. I
also pray for the weather to get
        better. Please God protect my family,
    my brother, and all the military
personnel. Also, please protect everything and everyone in the world.

—Kerrie, age 13

Brennan, age 10

Haley, age 9

I pray for
my grandpa.
Amen.

—Nicholas, age 6

Dear God,
Bless my Grandpa who is hurting
and bless my Grandma so that she can feel
better. She is hurting right now and asking
for help. Please bless her so that she will be
able to talk to You. Please bless my
Grandpa and Grandma. Amen.

—Ashleigh, age 10

Cassie, age 9

I pray for Jesus.

—Kyle, age 6

Adam, age 13

Dear God,
What I thought of heroes before September 11 were sports players like Sammy Sosa, Mark McGuire, and Scott Rolen. Not anymore. They may be my second best heroes but my #1 heroes are the people in the armed forces, medical doctors, firemen, policemen, and the office men and women from the World Trade Center. Thank You, God, for giving them the courage to fight for other peoples' lives and their own lives.

—Brad, age 11

IV. Pleaful Whispers

Casey, age 11

Shayna, age 10

Dear God,
Please help my Mom get her job back so we can go to Florida
—Meggan, age 8

Oh God,
Please take care of my Mom as she travels. Take care of her when she is on an airplane and take care of her when she is driving in a car. Thank You, Lord. Amen.
—Riley, age 8

Skylar, age 11

Dear God,
   I would like to pray for all of the poor people. Maybe some of the wealthy people could share some of their money with them.

–Jordan, age 10

Andy, age 7

Nathan, age 6

Dear God,
Please send good health to my aunt who has been sick from the cold.

—Zevon, age 13

Xyan, age 11

Dear God,
I want my sick friend to get back to school.

—Maddison, age 6

Dear God,
Please help my neighbor not kill my cat this summer.

—Caytee, age 11

Luke, age 10

Maisie, age 10

Dear God,
    Please save my teddy bear from fire and smoke.
    —Robbie, age 7

Dear God,
    Thank You for everything You gave me and the things You didn't.
    Please take care of my Mother.   —TJ, age 8

Erica, age 7

Regina, age 7

Oh God,
Please help me to not get sick. Please make sure I don't get sick. Please. Amen.
–Megan, age 8

Lord,
I love my dog. Thank You for giving me such a good dog. I love him. Please don't let him die. Let him be happy.
–Ross, age 12

Tiffany, age 9

Dear God,
Help me to be strong today since I don't feel good. Help me, God.
Love,
—Kyle, age 8

Ashley, age 7

V. Prayerful Whispers

Layne, age 11

Veronica, age 13

O God,
Thank You for the things I need. The things I want do not matter. I have put faith in You that can help me trust You.
Now and then I will need You and the Holy Spirit to help me choose.

—Jackson, age 9

O God,
Please don't let tornadoes come. Instead let trees grow and bees come. Let flowers bloom and not too hot let the sun shine. On Easter let it be sunny. Amen.

—David, age 9

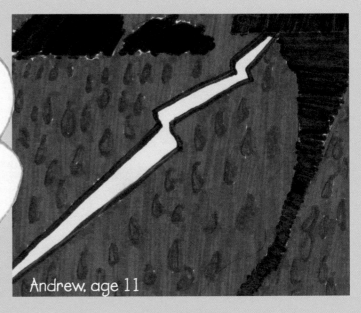

Andrew, age 11

Dear Heavenly Father,
    I thank You that this tragedy has only happened twice, and ask that it may never happen again. (Columbia Space Shuttle)
    I ask that you make the mourning for the families of the astronauts short and bring their pain to an end. In Your name, Amen.

—Jacob, age 14

Jacob, age 14

Nicholas, age 6

I love You, God. Please listen to our hearts and listen to the prayers of every-body. I want to praise You, God. Please take care of everybody. Thank You, God for giving us snow and pres-ents. I like You God because You love everybody.

—Amber, age 5

Dear Lord,
Forgive all my sins that I have done today. I want You to bless my friends and my family. We ask this in Your holy name. Amen

—Keisha, age 8

Luke, age 6

Dear God,
I am thankful for my friends and family.
I am thankful for all of the people I
know and all of the good things in my life. I am
thankful that I do not have to live out on the
streets and that my family has money. I
am thankful that I am able to go to church.

—Adam, age 13

Dear God,
Thank You for every-
thing I have today. I am
especially thankful for my
friends and family. Thank
You for all You have done
for me.

—Josh, age 12

Emma, age 9

Prayer of Thanksgiving

Thank You so much for my family and for my health. Some people don't even have what we have. There are people in Haiti that only have one water faucet for about every 3,000 people! People these days are so wasteful! God, thank You for everything that I have and I am very fortunate.

—Veronica, age 13

My Family

Lisa, age 14

My God,

I pray for the people who might be sick or ill. I pray for the people who do not have anyone in their lives. I pray for the people who bring money for the poor. I pray that people will not sin or turn their backs from God. I pray for people who are giving all their money they have and I hope they have a good life. I ask this in Jesus' name. Amen.

—Matthew, age 9

Emma, age 9

Thank You God,
Thank You for not making life easy,
Thank You for always being there.
Thank You for not making me gorgeous,
Thank You for the burdens I bare.
Thank You for all of the second chances.
Thank You for all of the "last times."
Thank You for always loving me,
Thank You for always having time.

—Katie, age 14

God Makes Our hearts Shine!

Zoe, age 9

VI. Powerful Whispers

Powerful
Prayers

Chris, age 11

T.J., age 8

Dear Jesus,
Please make me feel better. I feel yuckey. Please heal all sick people. Amen.

—Haley, age 8

Dear God,
Will You help my cousin because he might need to fight in the war. Make everyone that is good safe and have peace in our world. Amen.

—Brooke, age 10

Hannah, age 7

Lord,
Please let there be peace on Earth. Help us be kind to all people, not just our friends. Please stop war and hatred in the world. Help us to see the good in all people.
—Dorothy, age 12

Austin, age 12

Brandon, age 8

Jessica, age 6

When we meet other people, God wants us to see and bring out the goodness in them. Jesus, fire of love, thank You for the gift of warmth.

—Alyssa, age 11

When I think of fire I see Jesus' fire of love. Jesus, thank You for loving us. When I see rainbows I think of the beauty of God. God, thank You for making the beautiful creation.

—Bret, age 11

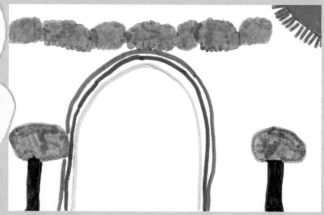

Nicole, age 10

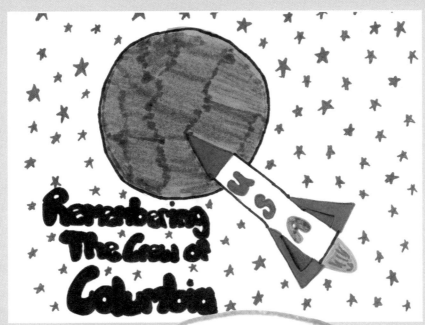

Teresa, age 14

Tears in Space

When the astronauts died, did they cry?
Did they cry for their families, their
friends, or their crew? Did they cry for themselves?
Did they pray to You? Did they ask for forgiveness?
Were they scared out of their mind? I would be.
I don't know about the rest of human kind.
Did You comfort them? Did You tell them every
thing would be alright? Are they with You now?
Are they watching me tonight?

—Katie, age 14

For Those Who Have Died

Dear God,

Please help those who died in the space shuttle. Give peace to those who lost a parent. We want them to live a happy life and find friendship. Help everyone who has died and their families. Amen.

—Summer, age 9

O God,

Please forgive me for all of the things I have done to hurt others especially my two brothers.

—Alex, age 9

Zeth, age 6

Mac, age 11

Almighty God,
We thank You for all You have done for us. You have helped me in many ways and answered many of my prayers. I would like to ask for Your help because You are all wise. God, I do not get along very well with my friends and family, and I ask You to help us find a common interest which I know exists. I ask this in Your name. Amen.
—Justin, age 14

When I see the United States flag, I think of God. Thank you, God, for making us a free nation.
—Mac, age 11

About God

God is our father. I think God is love. I think God wears a white cloth. I think God has brown hair and a mustache. I think God looks like a person. I think God is looking down on us every day. I know God loves us. God made us. I wouldn't have a dog or a cat if God didn't make them.

I think God is an angel. God helped me find my dog because I prayed. I think God made the weather. I am very thankful for God.

–Michaela, age 7

Alyssa, age 11

Mac, age 10

When I see the beautiful sun, I think of the light God gave us, because He is the light of the world. Please, God, keep shining Your light on us. In my classroom we pray. It helps me when there is a test. Thank You, God, for helping me relax.
—Bret, age 11

Please God, Make this flood go away, don't make it come back another day.

Quinton, age 11

Thank you God for allowing us to pray like Notre Dame students.

—Mac, age 11

Mac, age 11

Clint, age 13

Oh God, I humbly thank You for the great many things that You have done for us. God, the family that You have given me is the greatest I could ever know. You truly care about me. I thank You for all the wonderful and mysterious things that You have given to the world. Amen.

—Justin, age 14

VII. Whispers of Jesus' Passion

T.J., age 8

Introduction:
O God, help us to take up our cross like You take up yours. Please help us to do stuff even if we do not want to do it. Help us to have courage, love, faith and strength to follow Your way. Amen.

—Riley, age 8

Jesus Is
Condemned to Death
Pilate said Jesus
had to die. Dear Jesus, help
me to do what You wish of
me and to not be afraid to
die when it is time. Thank
You for forgiving our sins.
Amen.

—Grant, age 8

Shayla, age 8

Jesus Takes Up His Cross

Pilate made Jesus pick up His heavy cross. Jesus had to carry a big load. Jesus, help me when I feel my work is too hard. Thank You for letting me spend time in prayer with You. Amen.

—Meggan, age 8

Meggan, age 8

Jesus Falls for the First Time

Dear Jesus, please be with me to help me be brave like You. I sometimes fall because I don't want to do something like going to my dad's house sometimes. Help me be strong. Thank You for giving me life. Amen.

—Macy, age 8

Brandon, age 8

Jesus Meets His Mother

I bet Jesus wasn't happy when He was carrying the cross. His mother was sad to see Him hurting. I find it hard to watch my mother when she has hard work to do. Make me stronger so I can choose to do the right thing and help my family. Jesus, thank You for everything You do for me. Amen.

—Shayla, age 8

Hannah, age 8

Simon Helps Jesus Carry the Cross

Look how hard it is for Jesus. He needed help so Simon helped Him. Jesus, give me help when I am tired and weak from doing hard things. Thank You, Jesus, for the talent I have for hard work. Amen.   —Curtis, age 8

Curtis, age 8

Veronica

Wipes the Face of Jesus

Veronica wipes Jesus' face because He is sweaty and has blood on His face. O, God, help me to help others by making a joke to make a sad person happy. I want every-one to be happy. Thank you, Jesus, for my family and for my dog, Spud. Amen.

—Megan, age 8

Megan, age 8

Jesus Falls the Second Time

Jesus gets tired, becomes weaker and falls. The cross is getting heavier. Somebody helps Jesus. O God, help me to stay strong in kindness and love. Thank You for giving me life and for the Eucharist. Amen.

—T.J., age 8

Jon, age 8

Jesus Meets the Weeping Women

I can see Jesus with the weeping women. I wonder what Jesus is thinking. You comforted the weeping women when You were carrying the cross. Please help me comfort people if they are crying because they got hit. Thank You, God, for giving me life. Amen.

—Kyle, age 8

Hannah, age 8

Jesus Falls
the Third Time

The cross is so heavy He falls for the third time. Dear Jesus, my chores are hard, but You give me the strength to do them. Thank You for providing food for everybody. Amen.

—Jon, age 8

Megan, age 8

Jesus'
Clothes Are Taken Away.
Look how hard it has
been for Jesus. They stripped
him bare. Dear Jesus, let me
have strength when something
is taken from me. Sometimes
I need trust when my sisters
pick on me. Thank You, God,
for the earth. —Jeffrey, age 8

Brandon, age 8

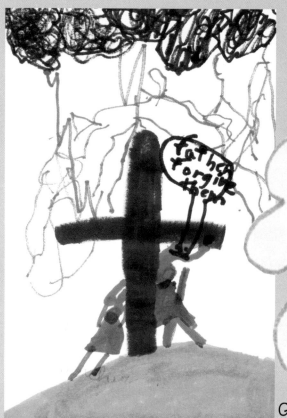

Grant, age 8

Jesus Is Nailed to the Cross

When Jesus was nailed to the cross, He was worried because He didn't know what was going to happen next. Dear Jesus, when my mother tells me to do some chores, help me do them. Thank You, God, for my family. Amen.

—Hannah, age 8

Riley, age 8

Jesus Dies on the Cross

Jesus, You died for us. When I am sick, I think I am going to die like You did. Help me to be strong when I am sick and weak. Help me so I don't hurt others by grumbling. We all know that You died for us and You will rise again. Thank You for my family and friends. Amen.

—Mark, age 8

Kyle, age 8

Jesus Is Taken from the Cross

Dear Jesus, when You were taken from the cross, everyone was really sad. You were put in the tomb. Two days later when you rose from the dead, I was glad. Please help me when I get scared. Thank You for giving me life. Amen.

—Brandon, age 8

Jeffrey, age 8

Jesus Is Placed in the Tomb

Jesus is put in a tomb. Do you think Jesus did the right thing? Take a good look at the cross. Lord Jesus Christ, help me to stand up to the kids that boss other children. Help me to hate Satan and his demons. Lord, please keep my mother and father safe. Thank You for the time I had in church. Thank You for my mother and father. Thank You for this day. Amen.

—Mark, age 8

Megan, age 8

Curtis, age 8

Jesus Rises From the Dead

Jesus gave His life for us. Three days later on Easter morning, Jesus rose from the dead. O God, help me to be kind and to sacrifice my turn for others. Help me to do what my mom and dad ask me to do. Help me to not be selfish. Thank You. Thank You for making me special. Amen.

—Haley, age 8

After two days, Jesus rose from the dead. Help me do well with my schoolwork. Thank You for my baby sister, Madison. Amen.

—Taylor, age 8

Taylor, age 8